The Book of
Cowboy Wisdom

The Book of
Cowboy Wisdom

Common Sense and Uncommon Genius
From the World of Cowboys

Compiled and Edited by Criswell Freeman

WALNUT GROVE PRESS
Nashville, TN 37205

ISBN 1-887655-41-7

The ideas expressed in this book are not, in all cases, exact quotations, as some have been edited for clarity and brevity. In all cases, the author has attempted to maintain the speaker's original intent. In some cases, material for this book was obtained from secondary sources, primarily print media. While every effort was made to ensure the accuracy of these sources, the accuracy cannot be guaranteed. For additions, deletions, corrections or clarifications in future editions of this text, please write WALNUT GROVE PRESS.

Printed in the United States of America
Cover Design by Mary Mazer
Typesetting & Page Layout by Sue Gerdes
Editor for Walnut Grove Press: Alan Ross
1 2 3 4 5 6 7 8 9 10 • 97 98 99 00 01

ACKNOWLEDGMENTS
The author gratefully acknowledges the helpful support of Angela Beasley, Dick and Mary Freeman, Mary Susan Freeman, Jim Gallery, and Cody Marley.

For Hunter Raquet

Table of Contents

Introduction

At the turn of the 20th century, Owen Wister published a novel called *The Virginian.* This romanticized portrayal of cowboy life became the prototype for the modern Western. One scene from the novel seemed to set the tone for all cowboy stories that would follow. In that scene, the Virginian, accused of being a poker cheat, laid his pistol on the table and snarled, "When you call me that, smile!" Those words, written a century ago, still echo today.

William W. Savage, Jr. observed, "The cowboy is the predominant figure in American mythology." Not surprisingly, this myth is a synthesis of fact and fiction. The old-time cowpuncher did lead a rowdy existence punctuated by brief periods of high excitement. But cowhands seldom enjoyed the glamorous lives portrayed on stage and screen. The work was hard, the conditions were tough, the hours were long, and the pay was slim. Out of this rugged land grew a spirit of backbone and a determination that lives on today.

This book catalogues the insights and humor of cowboy wisdom. It is a collection of quotations and sayings from cowpokes, lawmen, outlaws, and historians (with a few movie cowboys thrown in for good measure). The ideas on these pages provide common-sense advice — on the range or off.

1

The Cowboy

From the earliest days of the Old West, a cowboy needed to be tough, courageous and good with a horse. His work was grueling, his hours were long, and his wages were meager. But the cowpoke's job provided certain benefits over and above a weekly paycheck. He enjoyed freedom, excitement, and the pleasure of earning a living on horseback. This was more than enough compensation to make the job worthwhile.

The *American Heritage Dictionary* defines a cowboy as "a hired man, especially in the western United States, who tends cattle and performs many of his duties on horseback." In this chapter, we'll round up a few more definitions of America's unforgettable mythological figure.

The cowboy spells romance
in American history.

Harry Maule

The American cowboy seems to be
something God created expressly
for North America.

Glenn R. Vernam

Most young cowhands take great pride
in their independence.

Fred Gibson

Cowboys are a hardy, self-reliant,
free and independent class, acknowledging
no superior or master in the whole universe.

Joseph G. McCoy

Today, being a cowboy
is more an attitude
than an occupation.

Bobby Bare

The Cowboy

The old-time cowboys began their life's work
by the time they were twelve, ridin',
totin' pistols and drivin' herds.

Jesse James Benton

Us cowboys wasn't respectable,
but then again we didn't pretend to be.

"Teddy Blue" Abbott

The cowboys have a language intelligible
only to the initiated.

Finney County Democrat, March 26, 1887

You don't often see a good farmer
that's a good cowboy.

Ray Holmes

In looking at the cowboy, we see a breed
as distinctive as the mustang horse
and the longhorn. He is, as a whole,
forever inimitable and unalterable.

Glenn R. Vernam

Every kid in the range country looks forward
to the day when he can cultivate a bowlegged
walk and hire out to a cattleman.

Archer B. Gilfillan

Having always looked for the brand on cattle
and horses, I always looked for some kind
of a mark on men. I never found anything
to compare with the people on the Plains.
I could always tell them, by their walk
or the way they looked.

Bones Hooks

You know a cowboy by the way he stands and
walks and talks.

"Teddy Blue" Abbott

Cowboy: a man with guts and a horse.

Western Saying

Nearly all cowhands
hate the idea of
walking anywhere.

Fred Gibson

The Texas cowboys were frontiersmen.
By virtue of their courage, recklessness of
danger, excellent horsemanship, and skill
in the use of firearms, they have been
an efficient instrumentality in protecting
the frontier settlements.

Harper's New Monthly Magazine, 1886

Only a man of unflinching courage and
quick movement could succeed in handling
animals whose characteristics were rather
those of the wild beast than those of a
creature bred for the sustenance of man.

Charles Moreau Harger, 1892

I could have made more money at some
other job. But if I had it to do over,
I'd still rather get a-horseback
and look at them cows.

Ray Holmes

You have to be an expert to ride into a herd
of cattle. I've seen the best riders dumped off.

Jesse James Benton

As long as the big outfits lasted, roping
and riding and pistol practice were
the hobbies of the cowboys.

Jesse James Benton

Nearly all first-class cowpunchers could
keep a tin can rolling with a six-shooter in one
hand and roll a cigarette with the other.

The Texas Kid

We can't see him from our green watery East,
but he is out there still, riding over miles of
hard, juniper hills. He isn't myth, just a man at
work who divides his days into spring and fall,
the two seasons of a cowboy's life.

Gary D. Ford

A cowboy was a riding employee.
He lost that title as soon as he became
a ranch owner.

Philip Ashton Rollins

To be a cowboy, the first thing is to like
to work cattle and horses.

Ray Holmes

Few cowboys ever owned much.
The primary reward of being a cowboy was
the pleasure of living a cowboy's life.

Stan Hoig

I've worked at a lot of jobs, but I've always
been a cowboy.

"Kid" Marley

I have been on the stage for 20 years and I love it, but do you know, really, at heart, I love ranching.

Will Rogers

The Cowboy

There is a little bit of cowboy and cowgirl
in nearly everyone.

Jane and Michael Stern

I didn't want to be a fireman nor a policeman.
And I didn't want to be a lawyer.
I always wanted to be a cowboy.

Tim McCoy

Cowboy stuff is merely a phase which boys
pass through, like playing Indians or soldiers,
only some of them never grow up.

Archer B. Gilfillan

At least once in every person's life, they had a dream of becoming a cowboy.

Rachelle L. Reavis

In characters, cowboys
are like never was or
never will be again.

"Teddy Blue" Abbott

2

The Cowboy Way

In the Old West, an unwritten code governed the daily affairs of life. Cowboys were expected to be honest and friendly; they were required to be courageous.

Movie sidekick Andy Devine developed a personal code that summed up the principles of honorable cowpunching. Andy explained, "I made a deal with my kids. If they'd do nothing to embarrass me, I'd do nothing to embarrass them. It worked out fine."

The following quotations summarize the unofficial requirements for membership in the informal brotherhood of honorable cowboys. If you follow this advice, everything will work out divinely.

The Code of the West was a gentleman's agreement to certain rules of conduct. It was never written into the statutes, but it was respected everywhere on the range.

Ramon F. Adams

The Code of the Range
was a way of doing
business, meeting others
and conducting oneself.

C. L. Sonnichsen

Cowards could not be tolerated in the
cowboy culture because one coward might
endanger the whole outfit in time of danger.

David Dary

Courage in days gone by meant taking
your own part, fighting your own battles.
On the range, you handled it yourself.
It was part of the code.

C. L. Sonnichsen

All honor to the Texas cowboy,
living or dead, with all his faults,
his virtues were many.

Edgar Rye

No coward could qualify as a true cowboy.

John J. Callison

Cowards never lasted long enough to become real cowboys.

Charles Goodnight

The Western man of the old days had little choice but to be courageous.

Walter Prescott Webb

Universality of courage was an earmark
of the cowboy trade.

Philip Ashton Rollins

The cowboy triumphed at a lonely work
in a beautiful and dangerous land. How?
Courage, strength, devotion to duty.

Paul Horgan

Cowboy: The chief qualifications
of efficiency in this calling are courage,
alertness, endurance, horsemanship,
and skill in the use of the lariat.

Joseph Nimmo, Jr.

Cheerfulness was part of the philosophy
of the range.

Philip Ashton Rollins

Cowboys were, as a rule, very good natured.
In fact, it did not pay to be anything else.

"Teddy Blue" Abbott

You can rub out cow trails with highways,
swap sagebrush for cities, and free grass
for filling stations, but you can't cure
the West of bein' "howdy country."

Old Cowhand

Never pass anyone on the trail
without saying "Howdy."

Code of the West

A cowboy is kind to children, old folks and animals.

Gene Autry

A cowboy must help people in distress.

Gene Autry

In a cowboy's camp, a stranger always
receives a hearty welcome.

Edgar Rye

Jesse Chisholm (Chisholm Trail) ...
No one left his home cold or hungry.

Chisholm's Gravestone, Geary, Oklahoma

A cowboy always helps someone in need,
even a stranger or an enemy.

Code of the West

A cowboy never takes unfair advantage — even of an enemy.

Gene Autry

A cowboy never betrays a trust.

Gene Autry

Never betray a friend or comrade
for the sake of your own gain.

Belle Starr

One of the most notable characteristics
of the cowboy is loyalty.

Texas Livestock Journal, 1882

We saw something then you all are not
going to see. I have seen a wagon loaded with
groceries, sitting in a wagon yard without
having anybody bother it while the owner
was gone. If you don't tie the auto down now,
when you come back it is gone.

Bones Hooks

For cowboys, there is a right and a wrong,
and there isn't a lot of gray area.

John Beckett

Cowpunchers, as a rule, played a reasonable, good and fair game of cards, especially around camp.

The Texas Kid

No real cowboy was a complainer.

David Dary

Don't complain. Complaining is what quitters do, and cowboys hate quitters.

Code of the West

You know the rules in a cow camp when they have no regular cook? When anybody complains about the chuck, they have to do the cooking.

Joe M. Evans

Keep it cowboy and keep it clean. Real cowboys are tough but not vulgar. You can tell them by the way they treat women. If a man doesn't respect women enough to clean up his mouth, he doesn't respect himself.

Georgie Sicking

Cuss all you want ... but only around men, horses and cows.

Code of the West

A cowboy never asks another cowboy
about his past.

The Cowboy's Code

It was a land of scattered ranches, of herds
of longhorned cattle, and of reckless riders
who, unmoved, looked in the eyes
of life and death.

Theodore Roosevelt

Any man who wasn't a worker, hardy, tough
and full of sand, wouldn't stick with the cow
business long enough to pay for his saddle.

Mari Sandoz

The majority of cowboys were true and
trusty men who developed generous and
heroic traits of character.

Joseph Nimmo, Jr., 1886

Chronic borrowers were none too popular
on the range.

Stan Hoig

The cowboy inhabits a world of his own.
He has his own language, customs, humor,
principles, ways of doing things and
manner of thinking.

Glenn R. Vernam

The cowboy myth is probably a more
influential social force than the actual cowboy
ever was.

David B. Davis

Most cowboys resent a sick spell worse
than a five-mile walk.

Fred Gibson

Fun was the main thing. A cowboy would
climb any obstacle to have a moment's fun.

Glenn R. Vernam

When we hit town it was our intention and
ambition to paint the town red. Two months
on the dusty plains made us thirsty and wild.

Nat Love

We cowboys take a bath
whenever we get a chance.

Bob Lucas

There is still a large class which looks
with horror upon the approach of manners.

Dodge City Globe, 1879

The old-time cowboys were a class
of pioneer we ought to be proud of.

John J. Callison

The cattlemen thought themselves free men,
the freest men who ever lived.

Bernard de Voto

The main thing for a cowboy is to stand
on his own two feet with the courage that
will insure his beloved freedom.

Glenn R. Vernam

Cowboys call no man master.

Theodore Roosevelt

Make me as big and
open as the Plains;
As honest as the horse
between my knees;
Clean as the wind that
blows behind the rains;
Free as the hawk that
circles down the breeze.

From the Cowboy's Prayer, Badger Clark, 1906

3

Wide Open Spaces

An old ballad sums up the cowboy's place of business:

My ceiling's the sky, my floor is the grass,
My music's the lowing of herds as they pass.
My books are the brooks, my sermons the
*   stones,*
My parson's a wolf on his pulpit of bones.

Out West, there were no time clocks, no office hours, and no traffic jams — just open space and lots of it. Not a bad place to work.

Out where the
handclasp's
a little stronger,
Out where the smile
dwells a little longer —
That's where
the West begins.

Arthur Chapman

The truth is that nobody knows exactly
where the West begins. The West is as much
a state of mind as of geography.

Oren Arnold

The West, where a man can look farther and
see less of anything but land and sky.

Will James

Eastward I go only by force;
but westward I go free.

Henry David Thoreau

I have always regretted that I didn't live
about 30 or 40 years earlier, and in the same
old country — the Indian Territory. I would
have liked to have gotten there ahead
of the barbed-wire fences.

Will Rogers

First there was the buffalo trail, then the
cattle and wagons went over the trail, and
now you have the paved highway.

Bones Hooks

It was still the Wild West, the Far West ...
a land of vast silent spaces, of lonely rivers,
and of plains where the wild game stared
at the passing horseman.

Theodore Roosevelt

It's all in where your priorities are. I'd rather
lay my bedroll out in a horse camp than a
fancy room. Been in a lot of houses that were
too clean. Why, some of those immaculate
housekeepers don't even know
what a wild rose smells like.

Georgie Sicking

In that land we led a free and hardy life,
with horse and rifle.

Theodore Roosevelt

I liked the looks of the country.
Everything seemed to be wild.
So I decided to be wild myself.

Caswell McDowell

I've always liked the mountains because —
well, the sons-of-guns are *home*.

Ron Willis

I felt the heaviness of the silence.
It was as if the big mountains were pressing
down on the country, crushing all sounds.
But some sounds survived, little sounds
and beautiful sounds, like a lark's song
and the rustling of the tall grass and
the whir of a blue grouse's wings.

John Upton Terrell

There was no Sunday. Lots of times a man
would not know what day of the week it was.
You lose time out on the range with just
a bunch of men for 90 days. It would be
just daylight and night.

Bones Hooks

It was over flatlands like this, stretching out
to drink the sun, that the larks sang — and
one's heart sang there, too. There was a new
song in that blue air which had never been
sung in the world before.

Willa Cather

Above all things, the plainsmen had to have
an instinct for direction. I never had a
compass in my life, but I was never lost.

Charles Goodnight

A man learned to tell where there was
water and where there was no water. He would
watch the birds and see which way they were
flying in the early morning. He learned that
the birds flew to water in the morning and
from it in the late evening.

Bones Hooks

I heard the hail long before it reached me.
I heard it first as a low ominous rumbling.
Then I saw it coming up the valley,
an immense dark blue broom swinging
from the sky and sweeping the earth.

John Upton Terrell

That rusty old rattler suddenly appeared to
me as something natural, native and honest,
belonging to the land that I belonged to.
It is a fellow creature I would not want
to see exterminated.

J. Frank Dobie

You could take me in a plane and drop me
just about anywhere. And I know that
somehow I'd make out. Maybe the American
cowboy represents the last of the free men.

Casey Tibbs

The inhabited part of a ranch, the part of it
on which people live, bears the same
proportion to the rest of the ranch
as a lighthouse does to the ocean around it.

Richard Harding Davis

There's nothing nicer than to ride out
on a good, stout horse among a bunch of
cows when they're all doing good,
looking over the nice grass and knowing
the cattle are all taken care of.

Ray Holmes

No man who ever lived upon the range,
in looking back on his life, regretted that
residential privilege.

Philip Ashton Rollins

The cowboy goes to the school of nature.

W. S. James

There are few sensations that I prefer to that of galloping over these rolling, limitless prairies, rifle in hand, or winding my way among the barren, fantastic and grimy picturesque deserts of the so-called Bad Lands.

Theodore Roosevelt

Wilderness was a source of great joy to the cowboy.

Baylis John Fletcher

Out here, one is truly alone with God.

Frances Boyd

Oh, bury me not
on the lone prairie,
Where the wild coyotes
will howl over me.

Cowboy Ballad

4

The Horse

In 1944, Gene Autry and his horse were romanticized with these words:

Autry rode as if he were a part of his horse, or the horse a part of him, but there was a deeper unity between these two. Neither man nor beast felt any need to depend on any other creature. They had learned to trust in no help but their own strength, courage, speed, wits and fighting hearts.

The Hollywood publicists may have gone a little overboard in describing the bond between ol' Gene and his trusty steed, Champion. But not much. Cowpunchers, past or present, real or mythical, depend upon good horseflesh. In this chapter, we'll consider the care and feeding of history's most widely used all-terrain vehicle: the horse.

The cattleman —
yesterday, today and
forever — admires,
respects and loves
his horseflesh.

C. L. Sonnichsen

Something happens to a man when he gets
on a horse, in a country
where he can ride forever.

William Brandon

The cowboy and his horse
were inseparable companions.

John J. Callison

He don't need no iron hoss, but covers his
country on one that eats grass an' wears hair.

Charles M. Russell

The horsemanship of cowboys is admired,
and deservedly so.

Peter Wright

You have to be more or less a horseman
to be a cowboy.

Ray Holmes

The Horse

There is an invincible spirit of horse
and man.

Dane Coolidge

No man by taking thought can add to his
stature, but by taking a horse he can.

J. Frank Dobie

A good horse is worth its feed.

Cowboy Saying

A good cowboy ought to be able to get
along with a horse. A horse fighter
is not a good hand.

Ray Holmes

A good horse is most important
to any cowboy, old or modern.

Jesse James Benton

The cowboy's life
evolved around the cow,
but he owed that life
to the horse.

Joseph G. Rosa

The Horse

The horse was the cowboy's constant
companion. Each cowboy had stories
of the ability, skill and understanding
of his favorite horse.

David Dary

Never even *bother* another man's horse.

Code of the West

It's all right to live on a horse —
if it's *your own* horse.

Walter Brennan

No better word can be spoken of a man
than that he is careful of his horses.

Jim Flood

Always tend to your horse's needs before your own.

Code of the West

There ain't a horse that can't be rode. There ain't a man that can't be throwed.

Saying of the Old West

The mustang craved to wear
no man's saddle.

Foster-Harris

Riding a bronc is like dancing with a girl:
You just fall into the rhythm. But you've got
to know your business. If not, you'll either
pop your gizzard or eat dirt.

Casey Tibbs

Saddle breaking a horse isn't a job to be left
to the womenfolk and children.

Fred Gibson

After horses are broke to ride, my theory
is that they enjoy people.

Ray Holmes

The Horse

The more you ride your horse after cattle,
if you take care of him, the better horse
he makes.

Jesse James Benton

The art of horse-sitting is acquired rapidly
if one keeps at it from daylight till dark,
day after day.

Agnes Morley Cleaveland

A ranch horse is somewhere between
a teddy bear and a good pocket knife.

Baxter Black

I'd a whole lot rather work with horses
than put up with some people I know.

Mike Gibbs, Farrier

The horse race was an ever-present and unfailing source of enjoyment for the cowboy.

Emerson Hough

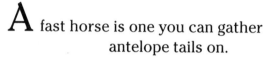

A fast horse is one you can gather antelope tails on.

"Kid" Marley

The expert cutting horse is just as anxious to start as any race horse at the starting gate.

Jesse James Benton

A cowboy was expected to saddle his own horse. Help was not appreciated.

David Dary

A good cowboy knows
the limits of his horse.

"Kid" Marley

Thaw out some old-timer of the Cattle Country
and ask him to tell you of horses that he knew.
His face will overspread with a reminiscent,
loving smile; he will say, "But of all the horses I
ever ran across, I knew one that was all horse."

Philip Ashton Rollins

As long as cowboys sing, "Old Faithful"
in the solitude of the night or in the glare
of the spotlight, so long will the horse
hold his place in the affections of man.

Rocky Lane

The love of a horse explains why there are
cowboys — not rough riders, or the
gun-decorated hero of the moving picture,
but earnest, everyday, hardworking boys
who will sit 24 hours in a saddle and never
whimper, but who "hate your guts" if you ask
them to plow an acre of land
or do anything else "afoot."

Frank Hastings

The Horse

Throughout the ages, a man on a horse
   has been the man respected and honored
            by the man afoot.

Fred Gibson

A man afoot is useless.

Jim Flood

It is an old saying on the Plains:
   A man without a horse has no business
            on the prairie.

H. M. Stanley, 1895

There were
only two things the
old-time cowpunchers
were afraid of:
a decent woman
and being set afoot.

"Teddy Blue" Abbott

Try to imagine
the Lone Ranger
without Silver.

Jane Tompkins

5

Gear and Garb

C. L. Sonnichsen wrote, "The cowboy uniform is a symbol of strength and virtue. It is something to live up to. It is, to some degree, sacred."

The following quotations describe the official uniform of the American cowboy: no loafers, no sport coats, no button-down shirts and club ties. Just hats, chaps, jeans, maybe spurs. And when it comes to footwear, it's boots or barefoot. Anything else would be sacrilege.

The cattleman feels himself apart from the rest of the human race, and therefore he wears a uniform.

C. L. Sonnichsen

Everything the working man on horseback wears, uses, or does has a logical purpose developed over more than a century of practical experience.

Glenn R. Vernam

Gear and Garb

In cowboy country, the fashions of apparel
do not change. The costume of the cowboy
is permanent because it is harmonious
with his surroundings.

Emerson Hough

The cowboys adopted a costume
in harmony with their occupation.

Edgar Rye

You generally can tell pretty much about
a cowboy by his clothes. You can be fooled
up to a point, but not too far.

Ray Holmes

A cowboy was covered from head to foot
in a protective costume that identified him
as distinctly as a knight's armor identified
its owner.

William H. Forbis

A cowboy moving across a board floor suggested the transit of a knight in armor.

Philip Ashton Rollins

The cowboy hat is perhaps the most popular character in Western fiction.

Lewis Nordyke

Along with saddle and boots, the hat
was the cowboy's proudest, most personal
possession. It warded off hailstorms and
low-flying branches; it could be used
to fan a fire or carry water.

William H. Forbis

The wide brim of the hat was not for
appearance. It defended from a burning sun.

Philip Ashton Rollins

Like a peacock needs feathers,
John Q. Cowboy needs his headgear.

Raymond Schuessler

Don't try on another man's hat.
It's almost as bad as getting on his horse.

Cowboy Hat Etiquette

Gear and Garb

The single piece of equipment the cowboy was fussiest about was his saddle. And small wonder. For months at a time, he sat in it all day and sometimes half the night.

William H. Forbis

Cattlemen can talk about saddles by the hour.

C. L. Sonnichsen

Once broken in, a saddle was like an old pair of boots that conformed uniquely to its owner's anatomy.

Michael Friedman

When you're riding all the time, get your own saddle and your own gear, so you can do what you want with it.

Ray Holmes

To sell one's saddle was a sign of poverty.

John J. Callison

The saddle was the cowboy's work bench and his throne.

Philip Ashton Rollins

Spurs were a necessary implement when on horseback and a social requirement when off.

Philip Ashton Rollins

A cowboy loves his hat and trusts his gun,
but he lives in his boots.

Jane and Michael Stern

You could always tell if you saw somebody
with their boots in the hatrack and their hat
on the floor, that they were from Texas.

Bones Hooks

A serious boot aficionado would no more
stomp around the dirt in them than you
would use an ancient pueblo pot to hold
your tuna salad.

Jane and Michael Stern

We used to make boots to fit a stirrup.
Now we make them to fit the gas pedal
of a Cadillac.

Cosimo Lucchese, Master Boot Maker

Back then, we went out in April. You carried everything you owned in a bedroll. When the grass started dying and the horses went to getting weak, we'd pull in around November.

Boots O'Neal

Nothing better than chaps has ever been devised for protecting a rider from cactus, barb wire, brush, rope burns, horse's teeth and sideswiping cow horns.

Glenn R. Vernam

A cowboy's clothing, though picturesque, was not worn for effect. It was simply best suited for the work at hand.

Philip Ashton Rollins

Every cowboy knows that the skin he saves may be his own.

Glenn R. Vernam

You can be mighty suspicious of a man in boots if he has an indoor complexion.

C. L. Sonnichsen

There will probably always be in the West a type of young fellow who cannot go out and drive the milk cows without buckling on chaps and spurs.

Archer B. Gilfillan

6

Cattle

Cattle can be as stubborn as the cowpokes who tend them — and equally excitable.

Texan Caswell McDowell noted, "Most anything you want to say about cowboys is true. But the important thing is, they take care of cows." In this chapter, we consider the noble animal that gives the cowboy his name.

Cattle

The cow became the companion of man
in his far wanderings, often the center
of his existence.

Mari Sandoz

The main course of Western history
is inextricably mixed with cattle.

Harry Maule

No cows, no cowboys.

Col. Edward N. Wentworth

The longhorn cow was a symbol of the
Wild West not only because of its independent
nature, but because of the respect it earned
by surviving the trail drives.

Jane and Michael Stern

Regardless of their color, longhorns
could run like deer, swim like sea lions,
and fight like catamounts.

Foster-Harris

Many an early Texan lived almost
as wholly from his cow as the Plains Indian
did from his buffalo.

Mari Sandoz

Our cattle shall also go with us.

Exodus 10: 26

Cattle became the circumference of our
universe, and their behavior absorbed our
entire waking hours.

Agnes Morley Cleaveland

The domestic cattle of Texas, miscalled
tame, are fifty times more dangerous
to footmen than the fiercest buffalo.

Anonymous 19th-Century Traveler

As long as a man called himself a cowboy,
his life centered on those thickheaded, panic-
prone creatures he referred to as cows.

William H. Forbis

Cattle

Cattle just naturally love music,
and many a herd that went up the trail snored
  to the tune of some cowpuncher's fiddle.
J. Frank Dobie

The steers stampeded in grand shape,
  the herd splitting up into a dozen different
  bunches. I finally got them stopped and,
    after singing a few "lullabye" songs,
    they all lay down and went to snoring.
Charlie Siringo

Orders were given to sing when you were
  running with a stampede, so the others
  would know where you were. After a while
  this grew to be the custom on the range.
"Teddy Blue" Abbott

Most big stampedes come off at night,
  and the worst ones happen when the cows
    have been asleep.
Dane Coolidge

In a general way, all cattle have their regular
places in a herd.

The Texas Kid

Never let a cow take a step, except in the
direction of its destination.

Jim Flood

For the stockman to be short of water
is worse than to be short of food.

J. M. Pollock

You can't fight a horse and work cows
at the same time.

Ray Holmes

Cattle

I woke up one morning
          on the old Chisholm Trail,
     Rope in my hand and cow by my tail,
  Feet in the stirrups and seat in the saddle,
I hung and rattled with them longherd cattle.
Cowboy Ballad

Nowhere are cowboys, both real and
          imaginary, more noticeable
          than on cattle drives.
Joyce Gibson Roach

The roundup takes us eight days —
     the most marvelous days of my life.
Luis Hernández

If there's anything that looks like a pest
or scourge to a cowman, it's a band of sheep
comin' over the hill.

The Texas Kid

The cowman will always mix it up with the
sheepman as long as there's open country
and cattle and sheep.

Will James

Cowpunchers and sheepherders have very
little in common. About the only time they
ever mix is when a bunch of cowboys try
to eat all the grub in a sheep camp.

The Texas Kid

Cattle

Longhorns could walk the roughest ground, cross the widest deserts, climb the highest mountains, swim the wildest rivers, fight off the fiercest bands of wolves, endure hunger, cold, thirst, and punishment as few beasts of the earth have ever shown themselves capable of enduring.

J. Frank Dobie

Nature intended for cows to run free.

Ray Holmes

The earth is full of electricity, and we all know cattle will draw electricity.

Jesse James Benton

Dad taught me that if
you think like a cow,
you won't need
your rope much.

Georgie Sicking

7

Toughness

The depiction of the old-time movie cowboy was, of course, glamorized. In fact, the life of the cowboy was — and is — a difficult one. As Harry Maule observed, "The story of the American cowboy is, above all, a story of struggle."

Ranch foreman Mike Gibson noted, "You don't graduate from college and become a cowboy. I tell people this is like playing for an NFL team. I need men as tough as tough can get." In this chapter, we consider a trait that is as indispensable to a cowhand as his horse, his hat or his boots. That trait is toughness.

Toughness

Driving a herd of twenty-five hundred
longhorns was no job for a cowboy
who did not like a hard life.

Earl Schenk Miers

Living according to Nature's simple plan
may cut down on a rancher's overhead and
upsets, but no amount of cooperation with
Nature can make his life easy.

C. L. Sonnichsen

It's a hard life, dealing with the elements, but
at the same time you have a lot of freedom.
Each day is like a new world.

Billy Paul Vinson

We felt the beat of hardy life in our veins:
the glory of work and the joy of living.

Theodore Roosevelt

The tougher the fight, the more important
the mental attitude.

Michael Landon

It was a hard land,
and it bred hard men
to hard ways.

Louis L'Amour

On the Plains, the great specter
       has always been drought.

C. L. Sonnichsen

Sometimes we have winter all summer
  and summer all winter. It's mighty regular
    about not raining, though.

Mark Twain

You cuss the hot, and you cuss the cold.
But something always keeps pulling you back.

Ron Willis

In this country, six inches of soil may be
  all that stands between cattle and the rock
    of hunger.

Gary D. Ford

Physical injury, ordinarily the gift of bucking,
allowed the average man but seven years
of bronco busting.

Philip Ashton Rollins

The roundup was the time when a fellow
had to sleep a-running.

Montana Ranch Hand

After long periods of storms and
sleeplessness, riders would sometimes smear
tobacco juice inside their eyelids; the sting
kept them from falling asleep in the saddle.

Bart McDowell

A Tucson bed is made by lying on your
stomach on the bare ground. It was allowable
to put your saddle over your head
as protection from any hailstones
larger than hens' eggs.

Jimmy Cook

The man who follows cattle is often dogged by heartbreaking difficulties.

Glenn R. Vernam

Hardships? There's no communication with
the outside world in case of emergency.
That and the rattlesnakes. We killed 12
last summer.

Jean Smith, Cowboy's Wife

A whole chapter could be written
on rattlesnake bites and their consequences
on horses, cattle and men.

C. L. Sonnichsen

We worked under the scorching midsummer
sun, when the wide plains shimmered and
wavered in the heat; and we knew the freezing
misery of riding night guard round the cattle
in the late fall roundup.

Theodore Roosevelt

It still gets 50 below in the Judith Basin.
When it gets that cold, you can hear a mouse
walking a half mile away.

Anonymous Old Hand

My Christmas one year was looking
at the Sears-Roebuck catalogue.

Walker Williams

The true substance behind rodeo has a lot
to do with hard work and competition.
Just good solid healthy competitive spirit.
And a lot of heart ... and heartache.

Doug Van Zandt, D.V.M.

Rodeo's a kind of rough life. I've been
in the hospital 11 times and had two major
surgeries. I've also had years when I hit the
big money. But even if I never made a nickel,
I'd still stay at it.

Wayne Orme

When a man climbs astraddle a giant,
snorting, quaking hunk of gristle and ire,
he'd best be a man of substance.

Sign in Man's Hat Shop, Albuquerque, New Mexico

Those with a touch of swagger had earned
it honestly.

Bart McDowell

In between the celebrating that many did at
the start and end of a cattle drive,
the cowhands had long hours of hard,
dusty work.

Wayne Gard

It's bacon and beans most every day.
I'd as soon be eatin' prairie hay.

Cowboy Ballad

On the range, the supply of good cooks
was always low and the demand keen.

Ramon F. Adams

A desperate cowboy may eat cactus,
but he won't like it.

Dane Coolidge

Hard work, not cleverness,
       is the secret of success.

"Kid" Marley

Glamour tends to dissolve in sweat.

Bart McDowell

If we never had any storms,
      we couldn't appreciate the sunshine.

Dale Evans

8

The Western

In 1902, Owen Wister published his classic novel, *the Virginian*, and the legend of the mythical Western hero was born. Eventually, Wister's vision of the Wild West was translated into a seemingly endless assortment of novels, films, comic books, radio shows and television programs. So great was the impact of the Western that when Douglas MacArthur met John Wayne, the general stuck out his hand and said, "Young fellow, you represent the cavalry officer more than any man who was ever in uniform."

Wayne's most illustrious mentor was the great director John Ford. Despite having directed a wide range of movies, Ford liked to introduce himself by saying, "My name is John Ford. I make Westerns." We're glad he did.

Men like Owen Wister, John Ford and John Wayne helped create the cowboy mythology that is alive and well today. In this chapter, we examine the movies, the men, and the myths.

The Western

The Western hero symbolizes the man of honor, the good man, the man of action, and is something that will, I think, be eternal.

Lindsay Anderson

The movies confront the grand themes on a simple stage: the stark background of the American West.

Eli Wallach

After the final winnowing of men, the heroes, the villains and the clowns emerge.

David B. Davis

The cowboys are the people who created the romance and the adventure of the Wild West. Theirs is the story I like best to tell.

Ken Maynard

People like Westerns because they always know who's gonna win.

Hoot Gibson

In our mythology, the cowboy era
is timeless.

David B. Davis

A word about pain: Westerns invite audiences
to undergo a considerable amount of it.

Jane Tompkins

I ride into a place owning my horse, saddle
and bridle. It isn't my quarrel, but I get into
trouble doing the right thing for somebody else.
When it's all ironed out, I never get
any money reward.

Tom Mix

The Western is about moving on.

Thomas McGuane

The Western remains, I suppose,
America's distinctive contribution to film.

Arthur Schlesinger, 1963

Westerns were to movies what the sports page is to the daily newspaper: the best part of it; the toy department.

Gene Autry

The "singing Westerns" are a little song,
a little riding, a little shooting, and a girl
to be saved from hazard.

Christian Science Monitor, April 9, 1944

The Western is the best type of picture.
It's action, mostly true. You have horses,
movement, background scenery, and color.
That's why it's interesting.

John Ford

Trying to single out one of my pictures is
like trying to single out a particular noodle
you enjoyed in a spaghetti dinner.

Gene Autry

The old-time movie cowboys shaped my
body and mind for all the years to come after.

Ronald Reagan

The great Western hero
    is the reluctant loner.

John Sturges

It's that fantasy of a guy solving a problem
   himself. He doesn't dial 911. He works out
    the situation himself. If he doesn't,
      he doesn't exist.

Clint Eastwood

I never smoked a cigarette in a picture.
  And I never entered a saloon except to deal
     justice to an outlaw.

Tom Mix

I never drank nor smoked in a picture.
 Kids came to see my pictures. I didn't think it
was right for them to see drinking or smoking
      on screen.

Ken Maynard

I felt that some of the Western stars of the
twenties and thirties were too perfect. I made
up my mind I was going to play a *real* man.

John Wayne

I started riding horses when I was seven.
Before that I rode mules. And I learned to play
the guitar from my mother and dad.
They played for square dances.

Roy Rogers

I tried to make the Western hero
a roughneck.

John Wayne

Maybe being an introvert gives me,
by sheer accident, a certain screen presence,
a mystique.

Clint Eastwood

I like to be active in a role and hate
namby-pamby heroines who just stand
around while men do violent
and admirable things.

Dale Evans

I can't act, I can't ride, I can't sing,
and I've got millions of dollars to prove it.

Gene Autry

You have two stars in Western films:
the man and the location.

Budd Boetticher

The main characters in some great Westerns
are often the landscapes. Monument Valley
has been the hero in more than one movie.

Thomas McGuane

Like a dream house, a dream horse provides
a setting for the Western hero.

Jane Tompkins

Nobody watches TV Westerns more avidly
than the cowboys.

Larry McMurtry

Rodeo, Western movies, country music —
no one can now draw a firm line between
the cowboy and show business.

Bart McDowell

Just when the Western seems like it's gone
away, someone else comes along
with a different twist on it.

Clint Eastwood

The Westerner is the last gentleman, and the
movies which over and over again tell his
story are probably the last art form in which
the concept of honor retains its strength.

Robert Warshaw

If movies could be
a religion, I think you'd
get more out of Westerns
than any other genre.

Budd Boetticher

9

Good Guys and Bad Guys

The life of the Western outlaw was not all it was cracked up to be. Upon turning himself in to the law, Jesse James' brother Frank summed up the futility of criminal life: "I have been hunted for twenty-one years. I have never known a day of perfect peace. I'm tired of running. Tired of waiting for a ball in the back. Tired of looking into the faces of friends and seeing a Judas."

Herein, we consider the exploits of lawmen and badmen. As we contemplate their words, a conclusion seems inescapable: crime doesn't pay. And it never did.

Good Guys and Bad Guys

In the cow country "law and order"
was a loose term.

Stan Hoig

A part of the frontier tradition was that
the line between the outlaw and the lawman
was thinly drawn.

Joseph G. Rosa

Cowboy justice was hard and not burdened
with technicalities.

Lewis Nordyke

Hear ye! Hear ye! This honorable court's now
in session; and if any galoot wants a snort
afore we start, let him step up to the bar
and name his poison.

Judge Roy Bean

The killer had his day, then came to a swift
and violent end. If the law did not get him,
another bad man did.

William MacLeod Raine

The gun was a necessity to the Western
frontier's rough and ready life.

William B. Edwards

Oh, dyin' was easy, for livin' was hard.
You died for a word or the turn of a card.

Ballad from the Movie "Bronco Billy"

Those outlaws changed their names
more often than they changed their socks.

Anonymous Pioneer Lawman

Cow country had its share of the mean,
brutal, crooked and vicious. But such
individuals never represented
the true working cowboy.

Glenn R. Vernam

Cowboys are, in the main, good men;
and the disturbance they cause in a town
is done from sheer rough lightheartedness.

Theodore Roosevelt

Cattle theft is still a thorn in the cowman's flesh, and will continue to be as long as cows are worth money and not too hard to steal.

C. L. Sonnichsen

Somebody else's stock was easier to round up and brand, unless you got caught.

Anonymous

In a harsh, waterless land, a horse was essential to a man's survival. Stealing a horse imperiled life itself — and thus the crime became a capital offense.

Bart McDowell

The horse thief asked for no mercy, because none was ever given.

Emerson Hough

A horse thief may be hung peremptorily.

Code of the West

Leave Your Revolvers at Police Headquarters and Get a Check.

Notice Posted in Wichita, Kansas, 1873

Never allow a man to get the drop on you.

Wild Bill Hickok

Texas was an aggressive country.
Every bush had its thorn; every animal,
reptile, or insect had its horn, tooth, or sting;
every male human his revolver.

Anonymous 19th-Century Traveler

Dodge City is one town where the average
bad man of the West not only finds his equal,
but finds himself badly handicapped.

Andy Adams, 1882

I have seen fast towns, but Abilene
beat them all.

John Wesley Hardin

I am a shootist.

Clay Allison, 1878

If someone outdraws you, smile and walk
away. There's plenty of time to look tough
when you're out of sight.

Old Cowboy Saying

When we arrived at the prison gate,
  I looked up and read in large letters,
"THE WAY OF THE TRANSGRESSOR IS HARD.
ADMISSION, TWENTY-FIVE CENTS." But I was
  on the dead-head list and went in for free.

John Reno, Outlaw

They say there'll be a great roundup,
  Where cowboys, like cattle, will stand,
    To be cut by the Riders of Judgment
  Who are posted and know every brand.

Cowboy Ballad

There's right and there's wrong.
You get to do one or the other. You do one,
and you're living. You do the other, and you
may be walking around, but you're as dead
      as a beaver hat.

John Wayne

The more ignorant you are,
      the quicker you fight.

Will Rogers

10

All-Purpose Advice

Cowboys are nothing if not opinionated. In this chapter, we consider a brand of common sense that comes straight from cattle country. If you're smart, you'll make it your brand, too.

The quickest way to double your money is
to fold it over and put it back in your pocket.

Old Cowboy Saying

Talk low, talk slow, and don't say too much.

John Wayne

A closed mouth gathers no boots.

Old Cowboy Saying

When in doubt, let your horse
do the thinking.

Old Cowboy Saying

Live so that you wouldn't mind selling
your pet parrot to the town gossip.

Will Rogers

Learn to take your work seriously
    and not yourself seriously.
Clint Eastwood

Don't wave at a man on a horse.
    It might spook the horse.
    A nod is the proper greeting.
Code of the West

A good fence has got to be pig tight,
    horse high, and bull strong.
Old Cowboy Saying

Work your horse harder
    than you work yourself.
Old Cowboy Saying

Don't wear your brain out trying
    to remember someone you don't like.
"Kid" Marley

If you can't do it with a little,
      you can't do it with a lot.

                        "Kid" Marley

Never put a hat on a bed or bunk:
      That's bad luck.

                    Cowboy Hat Etiquette

Admire a big horse, saddle a small one.

                    Old Cowboy Saying

We must take the bull by the tail
      and look the situation square in the face.

                    Lyndon B. Johnson

Oil saddles at least once a year.

Ray Holmes

Grant that I may not criticize my neighbor
until I have walked a mile in his moccasins.

Indian Prayer

If you lose your temper, you lose.

"Kid" Marley

After you pass someone on the trail,
don't look back at him. It implies
you don't trust him.

Code of the West

The man who sits straight on his horse
rides farther with less fatigue.

W. S. James

If you want to keep the herd moving,
put your two best men on the point.

Oscar Thompson

When cutting cattle, cut them downhill
with your back to the sun.

Oscar Thompson

Always keep your word. A gentleman never
insults anyone unintentionally. Don't look
for trouble, but if you get into a fight,
make sure you win it.

John Wayne

Every obstacle is only a weakness
in your mind. Greatness is inside you,
if you only believe.

Gary Leffew

It's not who you are, who you know, or what
you've done in the past — it's how good
you ride right now that counts.

Ronny Kitchens

Don't lose confidence in yourself, don't
allow any gambling in camp, and above all,
don't leave your herd for anything.

Oscar Thompson

Don't be afraid to go after what you want to do and what you want to be. And don't be afraid to pay the price.

Lane Frost

You'll never break a horse if you're sittin' on the fence.

Cowboy Saying

Never get up before breakfast. If you have
to get up before breakfast, eat breakfast first.

Old Cowboy Saying

Never wake another man by shaking
or touching him: He might wake up suddenly
and shoot you.

Code of the West

Spend your life doing something
you believe in.

Charlie Daniels

We are all here for a spell;
get all the good laughs you can.

Will Rogers

11

Observations on Cowgirls, Rattlesnakes, The Last Roundup, and Other Inevitabilities of Cowboy Life

We conclude with a hodgepodge of cowboy wit and wisdom. Enjoy.

The cowboy was simply part of the West.
He who did not understand the one
could never understand the other.

Emerson Hough

Cowboys resemble each other much more
than they resemble outsiders.

Theodore Roosevelt

The cowboy's life resembled the Indian's
more than any other.

Paul Horgan

The old-time working cowboys constituted
one of the most motley collections
of daredevils ever assembled.

Charles W. Towne

Most cowhands are forever practicing the
art of roping ... it's an occupational disease.

Fred Gibson

The average cowboy was a bit ruthless
in his treatment of grammar.

Philip Ashton Rollins

A cowboy doesn't talk much;
he saves his breath for breathing.

Code of the West

Oh, to be a cowboy!
To ride the high lonesome, to strum a guitar
with good companions, to eat chili and
sourdough biscuits from a tin plate, and to
sleep at night under a million stars by the
crackle of a campfire as coyotes
wail their desert serenade!

Jane and Michael Stern

Keep him, keep him forever:
Next to the wild Indian, the cowboy is our
most interesting American citizen.

Oren Arnold

The problem is to fashion one's existence,
which is difficult because so many people
want to fashion it for you.

Jack Palance

The secret of happiness is being yourself.

Dan Blocker

There's no greater, no happier life
in the world than that of the cattleman.

Will Rogers

You've got to be lucky, but then you've got
to be able to take advantage of your luck.

Chuck Conners

If you're not having fun, you're not doing
your job right.

Cowboy Jack Clement

What this country needs
is dirtier fingernails
and cleaner minds.

Will Rogers

To understand ranch lingo, all you have to do
is to know in advance what the other feller
means and then pay no attention
to what he says.

Philip Ashton Rollins

A real cowboy always saddles his own horse
and kills his own snakes.

"Kid" Marley

Without question the cook is the most
important man in any ranch outfit.

Ramon F. Adams

Words are inadequate to express the
admiration and respect the cowboys had
for those old-time ranchwomen.

Anonymous Southwestern Frontiersman

A cowgirl is a female whose life is or was for a significant part influenced by cattle, horses, and men who dealt with either or both.

Joyce Gibson Roach

Nothing short of a woman bound for outer space aboard a rocket would seem a likely candidate to replace the cowgirl. It's an interesting coincidence that the first female rocket rider's name should be Sally Ride.

Joyce Gibson Roach

I just can't get men to work as cowboys now. Most of the seasonal help I get is girls. That's right. In summer, most of my cowboys are girls.

Van Irvine

As long as the cowboy rides, the cowgirl rides with him.

Joyce Gibson Roach

I regard my experience, when I lived
and worked with my own fellow ranchmen
on what was then the frontier, as the most
important educational asset of all my life.

Theodore Roosevelt

I wish I could have lived my life drinking out
of a gourd instead of a paper envelope.

Will Rogers

Folks are not any harder to get along with
in one place than another.

"Kid" Marley

Tomorrow comes to us at midnight very clean.
It's perfect when it arrives, and it puts itself
in our hands and hopes we've learnt
something from yesterday.

John Wayne

If you can't stand to be alone,
    you'll never make it as a cowboy.

Dick Sayers

When a fellow ain't got much mind,
    it don't take him long to make it up.

Will Rogers

There is a giant asleep within every man.
When that giant wakes, miracles happen.

Max Brand

To love children is to love God.

Roy Rogers

You were born and can't help it
and you'll die the same way.

"Kid" Marley

Perhaps I may yet die with my boots on.

Wild Bill Hickok

Hickok died with his boots on, August 7, 1876

Whoever heard of a cowboy with ulcers?

Ramon F. Adams

There's always the next cowboy,
always another spring.

Gary D. Ford

If we think of the many possible heroes we might have had — then we can be thankful for our cowboy. We could have chosen worse.

David B. Davis

When I die you can skin me and put me
 on top of Trigger, and I'll be happy.
Roy Rogers

Yer dern tootin'!
Gabby Hayes

Thus ever it is in this world of ours
 The brightest light will fail
 Then a tear in the eye and an aching heart
 When we come to "The End of the Trail."
Anonymous Calendar Cover

Head 'em up, move 'em out.
Trail Boss, "Rawhide"

Sources

"Teddy Blue" Abbott 18, 19, 28, 36, 73, 92
Andy Adams 125
Ramon F. Adams 30, 107, 142, 146
Clay Allison 125
Lindsay Anderson 110
Oren Arnold 51, 139
Gene Autry 37, 38, 39, 40, 112, 113, 115
Bobby Bare 17
Judge Roy Bean 120
John Beckett 40
Jesse James Benton 18, 23, 62, 68, 69, 96
Baxter Black 68
Dan Blocker 140
Budd Boetticher 116, 118
Ward Bond 148
Frances Boyd 57
Max Brand 145
William Brandon 61
Walter Brennan 64
John J. Callison 32, 47, 61, 82
Willa Cather 53
Arthur Chapman 50
Agnes Morley Cleaveland 68, 91
Cowboy Jack Clement 140
Chuck Conners 140
Jimmy Cook 103
Dane Coolidge 62, 92, 107
Charlie Daniels 136
David Dary 32, 42, 64, 69
Henry David Thoreau 51
David B. Davis 45, 110, 111, 147
Richard Harding Davis 55

WG

About the Author

Criswell Freeman is a Doctor of Clinical Psychology living in Nashville, Tennessee. He is the author of *When Life Throws You a Curveball, Hit It* and *The Wisdom Series* from WALNUT GROVE PRESS.

About Wisdom Books

Wisdom Books chronicle memorable quotations in an easy-to-read style. Written by Criswell Freeman, this series provides inspiring, thoughtful and humorous messages from entertainers, athletes, scientists, politicians, clerics, writers and renegades. Each title focuses on a particular region or area of special interest.

Combining his passion for quotations with extensive training in psychology, Dr. Freeman revisits timeless themes such as perseverance, courage, love, forgiveness and faith.

"Quotations help us remember the simple yet profound truths that give life perspective and meaning," notes Freeman. "When it comes to life's most important lessons, we can all use gentle reminders."

The Wisdom Series
by Dr. Criswell Freeman

Regional Titles

Wisdom Made in America	ISBN 1-887655-07-7
The Book of Southern Wisdom	ISBN 0-9640955-3-X
The Wisdom of the Midwest	ISBN 1-887655-17-4
The Wisdom of the West	ISBN 1-887655-31-X
The Book of Texas Wisdom	ISBN 0-9640955-8-0
The Book of Florida Wisdom	ISBN 0-9640955-9-9
The Book of California Wisdom	ISBN 1-887655-14-X
The Book of New York Wisdom	ISBN 1-887655-16-6
The Book of New England Wisdom	ISBN 1-887655-15-8

Sports Titles

The Golfer's Book of Wisdom	ISBN 0-9640955-6-4
The Putter Principle	ISBN 1-887655-39-5
The Golfer's Guide to Life	ISBN 1-887655-38-7
The Wisdom of Southern Football	ISBN 0-9640955-7-2
The Book of Stock Car Wisdom	ISBN 1-887655-12-3
The Wisdom of Old-Time Baseball	ISBN 1-887655-08-5
The Book of Football Wisdom	ISBN 1-887655-18-2
The Book of Basketball Wisdom	ISBN 1-887655-32-8
The Fisherman's Guide to Life	ISBN 1-887655-30-1
The Tennis Lover's Guide to Life	ISBN 1-887655-36-0

Special Interest Titles

The Book of Country Music Wisdom	ISBN 0-9640955-1-3
Old-Time Country Wisdom	ISBN 1-887655-26-3
The Wisdom of Old-Time Television	ISBN 1-887655-64-6
The Cowboy's Guide to Life	ISBN 1-887655-41-7
The Wisdom of the Heart	ISBN 1-887655-34-4
The Guide to Better Birthdays	ISBN 1-887655-35-2
The Gardener's Guide to Life	ISBN 1-887655-40-9
Minutes from the Great Women's Coffee Club (by Angela Beasley)	ISBN 1-887655-33-6

Wisdom Books are available through booksellers everywhere.
For information about a retailer near you, call 1-800-256-8584.